GROWING AND CHANGING CITIES

BY KRISTIN CASHORE

Editorial Offices: Glenview, Illinois • Parsippany, New Jersey • New York, New York

Sales Offices: Needham, Massachusetts • Duluth, Georgia • Glenview, Illinois
Coppell, Texas • Sacramento, California • Mesa, Arizona

In the late 1800s and early 1900s, urbanization contributed to the rapid growth of cities in the United States.

Moving to the Cities

The population of the United States had grown all through the 1800s. However, in the late 1800s, there was more changing than just an increase in numbers. Where people lived, how they lived, and where they came from began to change too.

The United States had always been largely a rural, agricultural nation. At least 85 percent of all Americans lived either on farms or in rural communities near those farms in 1850. Farms were usually small, and most people could only raise enough food for themselves. Farmers had to hire a lot of extra workers if they wanted to raise enough crops to provide food for nearby towns.

In the late 1800s people who had lived in the country all their lives started moving to the city. This move from rural areas to cities, or **urbanization**, would change the United States. The country was becoming a nation of city dwellers. But why was this happening?

People from rural areas were moving to the cities to find jobs. In the 1800s **mechanization** had revolutionized farming. Machines now did the work that people once did by hand. Farmers could now feed far more people than ever before. This meant that suddenly a lot of farm workers were without jobs.

In the cities, factories were hiring many workers. There were a lot of jobs in the cities.

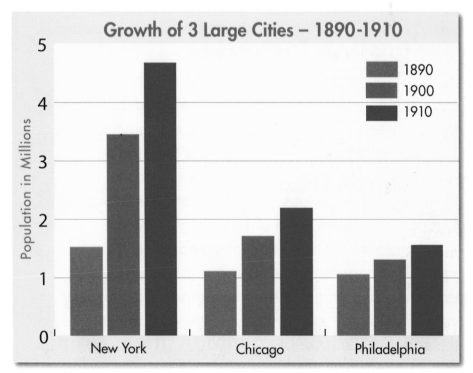

Almost all cities in the United States grew during this period, but some cities grew more than others.

The Know-Nothing Party held meetings to try to stop immigrants from taking American jobs.

Immigration Increases

People in other countries also noticed that there were a lot of jobs in America's cities. Between 1890 and 1910 more than 10 million immigrants flooded into the country. Never before had so many come to the United States in such a short period of time. This increased the size of the cities.

There were a lot of jobs, but there were not enough for everyone. Immigrants were often willing to work for lower wages, which meant they took jobs away from American workers. This angered many workers. Labor organizations and other groups often tried to keep immigrants from entering the country. The Know-Nothing Party protested against immigrants in the early 1850s.

Job shortages and protestors were not the only problems in the cities, however. People would soon have to face a wide range of issues, as populations continued to grow.

Opportunities and Difficulties

For most immigrants, the United States was seen as the land of freedom and hope for a better life. Because of increased opportunities, many poor people, both Americans and immigrants, did improve their lives during this period. They worked hard, and many succeeded. Some even became very wealthy.

With more people earning and spending money, more opportunities opened up. America became the most productive nation in the world. However, not every story was a success story. Also, the rapid growth of cities was creating new problems.

This photograph shows an Italian immigrant family in their home.

Many immigrants and rural poor who had come to the city could not escape poverty. Those who did not have skills or an education often had to take low-paying jobs. As more people arrived, housing became harder to find. Buildings were divided into smaller and smaller apartments, and large families often crowded into these tiny **tenements**. New tenement buildings were built quickly. Some were badly constructed.

Cities were growing too fast! Garbage removal could not keep up with the growth. Soon streets and rivers were filthy and unsafe. There were also few parks and not enough police or firefighters.

Because so many people were living so closely together, diseases spread quickly. Epidemics of polio, tuberculosis, smallpox, cholera, and typhoid fever killed thousands of people. An **epidemic** is the rapid spreading of a disease.

One problem of rapid urban growth was a lack of facilities for children, both for play and for school.

This political cartoon shows "Boss" Tweed welcoming a cholera epidemic. Political machines benefited from the suffering of others.

Political Machines Gain Strength

The cities' problems helped political machines gain strength. A political machine is an organization that controls votes to gain power. Political machines promised immigrants that they would help them if they had their vote. Once elected, these candidates did what the political machine told them to do.

A powerful political machine in New York City was Tammany Hall. Perhaps the most famous Tammany leader was "Boss" William M. Tweed, who bribed leaders and cheated people out of money.

Although most political machines were dishonest, many immigrants wanted their help. They believed someone was taking their side.

People Look for Real Solutions

City and federal governments worked hard trying to solve the problems in the growing cities. Individuals and organizations helped create solutions too. Organizations such as the YMCA, YWCA, and the Salvation Army—still well-known today—got started during this time. Immigrants who had succeeded formed groups that offered help to others coming from their respective homelands.

Scoring Points for Health

James Naismith worked at the YMCA in Springfield, Massachusetts and later taught college. He believed that exercise was important for health. He also thought it should be fun. He was worried because city children had little chance for exercise during the winter. So in 1891, with a leather ball and two peach baskets, he created a new game—basketball. The popularity of basketball spread across the country and around the world.

James Naismith invented the game of basketball to give city children something they could play indoors during the winter.

This laboratory was set up by 27-year-old Joseph Kinyoun, a doctor who wanted to study diseases that were epidemic in the United States.

People worked to improve public health. In 1870 Congress created a national health agency. New immigrants arriving in the late 1800s were checked for contagious diseases. Authorities treated the sick before letting them move into the cities.

In New York City, Dr. Joseph Kinyoun set up a laboratory in 1887. There he could study the contagious diseases that were killing so many people. In 1891 Kinyoun moved his laboratory to Washington, D.C. In time, the small laboratory grew into the National Institutes of Health.

Jane Addams started her famous **settlement house**, Hull House, in Chicago in 1889. Jacob Riis, an immigrant from Denmark, published a book of photographs titled *How the Other Half Lives* in 1890. The book's pictures of the urban poor had a powerful effect. It helped persuade New York State to pass a law in 1901 to make tenements more safe.

Growing Pains

Efforts were being made to improve health and education. Many people were working to make life better for the poor and to create cleaner, prettier cities. But cities were still running out of space.

People needed more than buildings to live in. They needed water, sewers, and garbage collection. They needed stores, doctors, and post offices.

Cities had a limited amount of land on which to build. As urban populations increased, space became a real problem. What could be done?

Building Answers

Two things came together to help cities create more space. The first was the invention of the safety elevator. Elevators were not new, but there was no way to stop them if they fell. So elevators were initially used to move products, not people. Then Elisha Graves Otis invented a braking system for elevators. If the elevator cable broke, this system would grip the tracks on either side of the elevator, bringing the elevator to a stop. People could now ride safely. Otis installed the first passenger elevator in a five-story department store in New York City in 1857.

The second part of the solution was steel. The Bessemer process for producing steel had been brought to the United States by Andrew Carnegie in the 1870s. Because of that, good steel was suddenly widely available. Steel and elevators were used in a new type of building called a skyscraper. Skyscrapers could be very tall because of the steel frame.

Otis developed the safety
elevator, an elevator that would
stop if the cable broke.

Skyscrapers were soon transforming cities all around the country.
This photograph of New York City was taken from the top of the
Empire State Building shortly after it opend in 1931. It has 102
floors! You can see many other skyscrapers that are not as tall.

The Great Chicago Fire destroyed Chicago's downtown
area in 1871. As a result, Chicago seemed like the best place
to experiment with skyscrapers. The first skyscraper, the Home
Insurance Building, was completed in Chicago in 1885. It was
just ten stories tall, but it was the tallest building in the country.
Taller buildings were soon being built.

Rivers posed another problem. Water transportation was the
main reason for the location of many big cities. Many cities
had grown up with rivers running either through, or alongside
them. The ferry boats used to carry people across these rivers
were getting overcrowded.

John Roebling, a German immigrant and building engineer, thought suspension bridges might help. Bridges that are **suspended** are hung from massive overhead cables stretched between tall towers at either end of the bridge. They could cross rivers without blocking them. Roebling combined new building methods with the strong, steel cable he had developed and built the world's first steel suspension bridges. The New York state legislature asked him to design and build a bridge that would connect Brooklyn and the island of Manhattan. Roebling designed the bridge, but he died before it was completed. His son, Washington, finished the bridge. Washington's wife, Emily, helped him after he became ill. When it opened in 1883, the Brooklyn Bridge was the longest bridge in the world.

The Brooklyn Bridge in New York City connected Brooklyn to the island of Manhattan.

Cities also began to create new forms of public transportation. Some cities built elevated trains, trains that were supported by steel structures that held them one or two stories above street level. New York's elevated train opened in 1870 and Chicago's in 1892.

Next, engineers began to consider going down, under the streets. Many cities began experimenting with this idea, but it was Boston, Massachusetts, that, in 1897, opened the country's first successful underground train system, or subway.

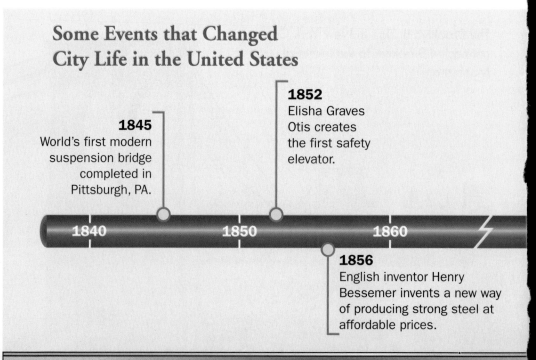

Some Events that Changed City Life in the United States

1845
World's first modern suspension bridge completed in Pittsburgh, PA.

1852
Elisha Graves Otis creates the first safety elevator.

1840   1850   1860

1856
English inventor Henry Bessemer invents a new way of producing strong steel at affordable prices.

Cities Yesterday and Today

During the late 1800s and early 1900s, the United States began to change from a rural nation to an urbanized nation. It was a period that began to create the modern United States. It gave rise to much of what we consider normal for big cities today, from traffic jams to subways to skyscrapers.

Many of the things that started during this time are still part of our lives. The first department stores opened during this period. The first shopping catalogs came out. Street lights began to line the roads. And as you read, elevators, skyscrapers, and public health programs were introduced.

Today, city governments still struggle to keep up with city growth. And today, immigrants continue to arrive, looking for opportunities in a land that still offers hope.

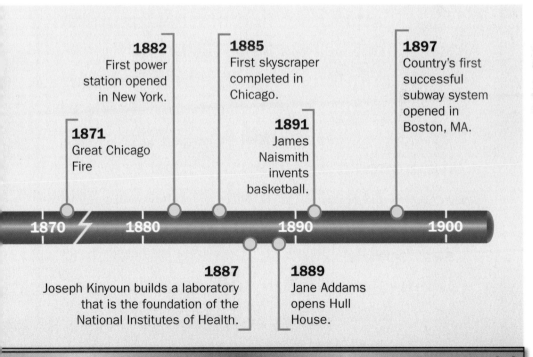

1882
First power station opened in New York.

1885
First skyscraper completed in Chicago.

1897
Country's first successful subway system opened in Boston, MA.

1871
Great Chicago Fire

1891
James Naismith invents basketball.

1870   1880   1890   1900

1887
Joseph Kinyoun builds a laboratory that is the foundation of the National Institutes of Health.

1889
Jane Addams opens Hull House.

Glossary

epidemic the rapid spread of a disease, so that many people have it at the same time

mechanization the use of machines to do work

settlement house a place that provides help for immigrants and the poor

suspend to hang by fastening to something above

tenement a building divided into many small apartments

urbanization the movement of people from rural areas to the city